Strange For Change
Vol. 1

Heather Scott

BookLeaf Publishing

India | USA | UK

Presentation by *BookLeaf Publishing*

Web: www.bookleafpub.com

E-mail: info@bookleafpub.com

ISBN: 9789360940966

First edition 2024

To DeBella Cayenani Roseayrn Renee',

Smile because you are beautiful because beautiful people make the world go 'round . You are My greatest accomplishment! I love you with all my heart, in a big circle that never ends. If I ever was a hypocrite in your eyes, I'm truly sorry. I really tried to do what I thought was always the "right" decision at the time.

ACKNOWLEDGEMENT

Mrs. Kim Tam was my first teacher in "real school" and first to truly encourage The Art of Writing. Thanks for having my 5 year old self's battle in the hospital with bronchial pneumonia published. I love you forever and always. Thanks for being a great Human!

PREFACE

..but why is my circular pizza cut into triangles and served in a square box?
..but why is the word abbreviation so long but means to shorten?
..but is the s or the c silent in scent?

Stop Brain!!! I just want to hit my trees and f'up this food!

SugaFoot, I Love You So

SweetPea I Love you so
Unlike the masses, we are a lot, the same
Gifted with a different outlook
And agree that we will disagree.

Fearless Goddesses
Obligations of the mother come first
Optimistically striving for betterment
Together we could, we can, we will

I know damn right; I had the dream.

Looking for ways to walk in purpose.
Openly and Free.
Visions of laughter and smiles.
Enough for us is so simple versus others.

Yearning to grow our own
Off the grid using what we have read about
Uplifting each other

Smile because we are Beautiful.
Oh, SugaFoot, I love you so.

Why Was I Blinded By You

What Did I see?
He was everything, simply
You would've agreed.

Waited for time to be spent
Amusing every positive sign
So enthralled with the essence of this man.

I know my worth though.

Being in love isn't supposed to hurt right?
Love; The smallest word that hurts so Big
I cry but I am wrong for that, for raw emotion
Nullifying my existence to a minimum
Damned to nothing because I ask Why's?
Everything you ever thought you wanted
Denounced loud because I just ain't shit.

But You know what You do to Me or She or 3
Your actions and words. You choose them.

Yearning for happiness was my downfall.
Only if you seen that in me,the unique one
Unicorn, but everyone's different.

Pulchritudinous

Physically Beautiful
Uniformly arranged
Lioness displays her will.

Consistent urges and desires fulfilled
Hedonism
Reaching into the depths of the Fire
I submit to you.

Too good to be true
Unique and mysterious
Dapperest Dame, one may say

Impression is impressive in this day
Nocturnal shenanigans
Orgasmically blended with relaxation
Unleashing carnal desires
Showing her attraction, the lioness lays down
awaiting ….more.

Moving Up Mindset

The difference is Passion....or maybe
motivation...
Mental to physical...the correlation
Dream higher than most.. escape the doldrums
The greater good being main focus... all the
while functioning for a sum
Difficulties bombard...hit with harsh realities
Come ahead like Ruettiger
Not losing sight..Strive to Thrive.

As If

High as the waterfall,
  My Hope
Peaceful as the stream,
  My Sleep
Light as the leaves,
  My Wings
It's as if I am Free.

Calm as the breeze,
  My Mind
Fluid as the water,
  My Mouth
Raging like the rapids,
  My Most Precious
It's as if You are Love.

Why Do I Question You

Why can I hear you talking or someone?
How do I know what man wrote was real?
You made us in Your image,so why the hate?

Don't You think I wanted to be Normal?
Or is this really some sinister joke?

I had to ask. Sorry.

Quite a variety of denominations, huh?
Unsolved mysteries, miracles, or cult lies?
Exactly who is right?
Sunday for some but Saturday for others?
Teaching of positivity should be focus right?
Instead day of worship is for best dressed?
Ones fill in pews for agenda and judgement?
Now go on GOD! Touch these folks soul.

You should try Jesus but wait, Not the Jews!
Or is their religion that says something other?
Unfortunately, now I'm confused.

Chronicles Of Accountability
Part 1

Acceptance of responsibility,
Coming up short in the modern day.

Cowards are the mass.
Ownership apparently was not taught.
Ugly lies chosen to be woven usually instead.
Neglecting and deflecting reprimand.
Taking the broom to sweep under a rug.

An ultimate epidemic of selfish.
Bold people concealing damaging truths.
Inclusive to 1 but 1's with 2,3, 4, or more
Loyalty loses sight when explorations aren't
shared.

It all catches up in the end.

Truth is the only thing that remains the same.
You should, at least, own up to those that matter.

With Spirit of 3

With the brawn of the lion,
walk fierce.
With the intelligence of the elephant,
walk with purpose.
With the quickness of the squirrel,
walk, no run, then dance, skip, and hop!

Rhyme Tyme Devyne

Why tip-toe like your walking on glass
Never take chances, never move fast
Sad little life dwelling in the past
The negative hits like a bomb's blast

Peace enlightening
Love's glow brightening
Beauty exciting
Life's mesmerizing

Beeeee-Cauuuuuse I got

Purpose in my stride
Sunshine in my eyes
Happiness in mind
You can't kill my vibe

Hanging Haiku

The noose made from rope.
Letting it control your life.
Be one with the rope.

Mind & Body

As I lay dying
Here at my worst
Mind & body, to one another lying

My tragedies screaming, in silence
Mind & body coerce
Visions become defiant.

Sleep is for the dead.
Mind & body tired but poised.
I'd rather fuck in Life's bed.

Hai-575 Fool-KuHead

Lil Me The Damn Fool
Because I wanted to prove
we all deserve love.

But I wanted you
to grow, build; that sense of safe
I could sleep peaceful.

But not so lately
maybe after them golds left
Moved them but I saw.

Walked around prideful
Happy was what I must Had
Because I Had time

Vibe switches with you
Your actions create distance
What else can I do?

The variety?
You could've had that with me.
I do play with both.

You don't want to share?
Sneaking over Honesty?
Who is that fair to?

6 and 9 Intertwine

that rolling stone
the one who swears he's all alone

that ghetto queen
like wild stylez was looking for on that red cd
with ya know, the man that liked to pee

that Mr. Earth
the third leg with mack daddy girth

that Mrs. Fire
sweat rolling down her breasts
breathing hard as a timpani beats below

Touching so slightly with tickle and pinch
Grabbing, pulling making the dome wetter

first embracing the appendage as a leech
then that fat cat wetting up the sheets
Orgasmic music; That Soul Beat.

ABCS and WTFS

Adults cause most trauma to children
Blinded By their way is right.
Child's place you must stay
Defeated by the ones who love you.

Evil occurs
Family covers up the most
God approved this to happen
How?
Incest ! Drugs! Whatever and whatever more
Just pray about it, right?
Kill myself instead?
Lord knows children don't deserve this.

Maybe this is why people think differently
Never really know what people go though
Only when they start talking about it
Putting words to their traumas
Quoting verses to find strength.

Rainbows and gold isn't in everyone's story
Some stories are nightmares.
Tragedy at its finest.

Ultimately choose to be a good human.

Vow to be passionate
Wholeheartedly love
Xenial and selfless actions
Yearn to learn
Zizz!

Disappointed And Dazed

Days like these
I wish I didn't remember
Some evils
And traumas.
People,
Places,
Objects, Opinions, Opposition!
Intertwined in this head.
Noise so LOUD!
Twisting
Every action and sound,
Devilishly, Until BOOM!

And Nobody cares.
Nobody has their own shit going on.
Demons eating everyone.

Definitely have hatred for some,
Animosity, whatever Nobody calling it.
Zoned out on the
Ever so evolving bullshit
Doned to us called Life.

Inalienable

I love yous, romance,
Nature, and waterfalls!

Adventure always awaiting me;
Living my best life.
Imagination fluidity,
Energy vibrating positive beats
Nurturing Soul; Music!

Actions matching words
Because integrity is of the most high.
Learning continuously;
Engaging a mind DNA is destined to destroy!

Unfukwitable

Underestimated and
Not your average human being

Fiesty but a good crazy
Unique, definitely with them
Killer cat eye's.

Weirdo! And I love it and him and her;
I love you hate me too!
Try me, bet you won't.

All aboard crazy train
Because this is one hella-amazing ride.
Lioness through and through
Equals Ruthless. Play with yourself.

Mad At The World

My mind yells,
Angry from built hurt,
Destroying the want to move forward.

And still I'm here;
Trying.

Truth is, I hate it.
How was I turn from a different cloth?
Emotions dead but yet so alive.

Why were weights put upon my shoulders?
Overcame most but ob so heavy I remain
Return back, snap back, Smile!
Life's journey hasn't much been my friend.
Drug, hit, and kicked me, but I will prevail.

Chronicles of Accountability
Part 2

Are you able to take ownership for your actions
now?
Caused enough damage to people yet?

Can you really own up though?
Or are we a tad bit narcissistic?
Unfortunately, most don't have the trait of.
brutal honesty
Narrative fits whomever you're with these days?
The Truth shall set you free ya know.

Am I the problem though?

Being the bearer of bad news?
Initialized that tough conversation?
Love yourself first though, I did always say that,
but am I..or am I putting you first.

Igniting some of the brightest fires

Trust the universe; take pride in your walk.
Your stride in Honesty will win.

Lift One Another

Listen to people and hear them
Inspire others
Feed children knowledge
Teach accountability

Own your indiscretions
Nurture your minds
Evolve into a better human

Accept what we cannot change
Never back down on your beliefs
Optimize your strengths
Take charge of your destiny
Heal from traumas
Express yourselves to the fullest
Realize above all, You are Amazing!